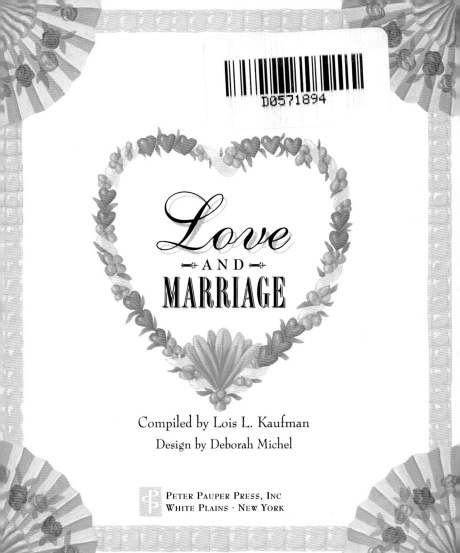

Love
❧ AND ❧
MARRIAGE

Compiled by Lois L. Kaufman

Design by Deborah Michel

PETER PAUPER PRESS, INC
WHITE PLAINS · NEW YORK

For Bill, my partner in
love and marriage

Copyright © 1994
Peter Pauper Press, Inc.
202 Mamaroneck Avenue
White Plains, NY 10601
All rights reserved
ISBN 0-88088-876-8
Printed in Singapore
7 6 5 4 3 2 1

Jacket background painting by Linda DeVito Soltis
Jacket inset painting by Grace De Vito

Introduction

*A*lan King says, "If you want to read about love and marriage you've got to buy two separate books." We don't agree with this point of view, but for the purpose of convenience have divided this Keepsake into sections on love and marriage.

*W*hen we think of love and marriage, all the old clichés come to mind: love makes the world go around; all the world loves a lover; sparks; fireworks; glowing embers. Perhaps there are so many clichés about love because, as Disraeli said, "We are born for love. It is the principle of existence and its only end." And, as we would like to believe, along with Richard Bach, "Real love stories never have endings."

L. L. K.

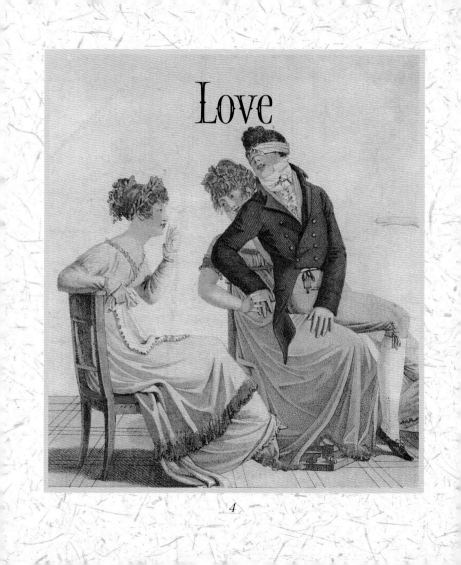

Love

$\mathcal{L}$ove is the master key that opens the gates
of happiness.

OLIVER WENDELL HOLMES

$\mathcal{T}$o love someone means to see him as God intended.

DOSTOEVSKI

$\mathcal{T}$o be a woman is to have the same needs and longings
as a man. We need love and we wish to give it.

LIV ULLMANN

$\mathcal{W}$hen one has once fully entered the realm of love, the
world—no matter how imperfect—becomes rich and
beautiful, for it consists solely of opportunities for love.

SOREN KIERKEGAARD

$\mathcal{I}$ have found it impossible to carry the heavy burden of responsibility and to discharge my duties as King as I would wish to do without the help and support of the woman I love.

EDWARD, DUKE OF WINDSOR

$\mathcal{L}$ove is not only a feeling, it is also an art. A simple word, a sensitive precaution, a mere nothing reveal to a woman the sublime artist who can touch her heart without withering it.

HONORÉ DE BALZAC

$\mathcal{T}$o fall in love you have to be in the state of mind for it to take, like a disease.

NANCY MITFORD

*R*eal love stories never have endings.

RICHARD BACH

*L*ove is much nicer to be in than an automobile accident, a tight girdle, a higher tax bracket or a holding pattern over Philadelphia.

JUDITH VIORST

*L*ife is a flower of which love is the honey.

VICTOR HUGO

*W*hen I fell in love, I had the usual symptoms. Insomnia, light fever, loss of appetite. It was like the flu, except the symptoms intensified in the presence of the intended.

SAM NEILL

I hold it true, whate'er befall;
I feel it, when I sorrow most;
'Tis better to have loved and lost
Than never to have loved at all.

ALFRED, LORD TENNYSON

*T*ake hold lightly; let go lightly. This is one of the great
secrets of felicity in love.

SPANISH PROVERB

*F*amiliar acts are beautiful through love.

PERCY BYSSHE SHELLEY

*L*ove is the last and most serious disease of childhood.

ANONYMOUS

$\mathcal{T}$he supreme happiness of life is the conviction of being loved for yourself, or, more correctly, being loved in spite of yourself.

VICTOR HUGO

$\mathcal{W}$e are born for love. It is the principle of existence and its only end.

BENJAMIN DISRAELI

$\mathcal{T}$he pleasure of love is in loving. We are happier in the passion we feel than in that we arouse.

DUC DE LA ROCHEFOUCAULD

$\mathcal{P}$latonic love is love from the neck up.

THYRA SAMTER WINSLOW

$\mathcal{L}$et me not to the marriage of true minds
Admit impediments. Love is not love
Which alters when it alteration finds,
Or bends with the remover to remove.
Oh, no! it is an ever-fixèd mark
That looks on tempests and is never shaken;
It is the star to every wandering bark,
Whose worth's unknown, although his height be taken.
Love's not Time's fool, though rosy lips and cheeks
Within his bending sickle's compass come;
Love alters not with his brief hours and weeks,
But bears it out even to the edge of doom.
If this be error and upon me proved,
I never writ, nor no man ever loved.

WILLIAM SHAKESPEARE

$\mathcal{A}$t the touch of love, everyone becomes a poet.

PLATO

*L*ove is a canvas furnished by Nature and embroidered by imagination.

VOLTAIRE

*T*o love means to embrace and at the same time to withstand many many endings, and many many beginnings—all in the same relationship.

CLARISSA PINKOLA ESTÉS

*T*he way to love anything is to realize that it might be lost.

G. K. CHESTERTON

*A*ll the world loves a lover, except those who are waiting to use the phone.

$\mathcal{E}$xperience teaches us that love does not consist of two people looking at each other, but of looking together in the same direction.

ANTOINE DE SAINT-EXUPÉRY

$\mathcal{W}$e love best in the days when we believe that we alone love, that no one has ever loved like us, and no one ever will.

JOHANN WOLFGANG VON GOETHE

"$\mathcal{G}$oing to him! Happy letter! Tell him—
Tell him the page I didn't write;
Tell him I only said the syntax,
And left the verb and pronoun out."

EMILY DICKINSON

It is not true that love makes all things easy; it makes us choose what is difficult.

GEORGE ELIOT

Love is a power too strong to be overcome by anything but flight.

MIGUEL DE CERVANTES

One of the best things about love is just recognizing a man's step when he climbs the stairs.

COLETTE

The perfect lover is one who turns into a pizza at 4:00 A.M.

CHARLES PIERCE

*L*ove is a friendship set to music.

E. Joseph Cossman

*T*alk not of wasted affection; affection never was wasted.

Henry Wadsworth Longfellow

*I*n love all of life's contradictions dissolve and disappear. Only in love are unity and duality not in conflict.

Rabindranath Tagore

*G*od did not create woman from man's head, that he should command her, nor from his feet, that she should be his slave, but rather from his side, that she should be near his heart.

Talmud

$\mathcal{N}$o cord or cable can draw so forcibly, or bind so fast, as love can do with a single thread.

ROBERT BURTON

$\mathcal{F}$or lovers, touch is metamorphosis. All the parts of their bodies seem to change, and they become something different and better.

JOHN CHEEVER

$\mathcal{L}$ove pleases more than marriage, for the reason that romance is more interesting than history.

NICHOLAS CHAMFORD

$\mathcal{L}$ove is never lost. If not reciprocated, it will flow back and soften and purify the heart.

WASHINGTON IRVING

*L*ove: the delusion that one woman differs
from another.

H. L. MENCKEN

*T*he ultimate test of a relationship is to disagree but to
hold hands.

ALEXANDRA PENNEY

*N*ever tell a woman you are unworthy of her love—she
knows it.

ANONYMOUS

*M*en adore women. Our mothers taught us to.
Women do not adore men; women are amused by men,
we are a source of chuckles.

GARRISON KEILLOR

*T*hey that love beyond the world can not be separated by it. Death can not kill what never dies.

WILLIAM PENN

*W*ho has not found the heaven below
Will fail of it above.
God's residence is next to mine,
His furniture is love.

EMILY DICKINSON

*L*ove comforteth like sunshine after rain.

WILLIAM SHAKESPEARE

A wise lover values not so much the gift of the lover as the love of the giver.

THOMAS À KEMPIS

$\mathcal{L}$ove doesn't grow on trees like apples in Eden—it's something you have to make. And you must use your imagination too. . . .

JOYCE CARY

$\mathcal{W}$oman would be more charming if one could fall into her arms without falling into her hands.

AMBROSE BIERCE

$\mathcal{A}$ll mankind loves a lover.

RALPH WALDO EMERSON

$\mathcal{T}$here's nothing a woman could do in bed that could possibly, in a million years, make her feel as guilty as eating four Clark Bars.

JUDITH VIORST

*C*aresses, expressions of one sort or another, are necessary to the life of the affections as leaves are to the life of a tree. If they are wholly restrained, love will die at the roots.

NATHANIEL HAWTHORNE

*P*eople talk about love as though it were something you could give, like an armful of flowers.

ANNE MORROW LINDBERGH

*W*e two form a multitude.

OVID

*T*o love a person means to agree to grow old with him.

ALBERT CAMUS

$\mathcal{P}$eople who are in love suspect nothing or everything.

HONORÉ DE BALZAC

$\mathcal{L}$ove preserves beauty, and the flesh of woman is fed with caresses as are bees with flowers.

ANATOLE FRANCE

$\mathcal{I}$t is not true that love makes all things easy; it makes us choose what is difficult.

GEORGE ELIOT

$\mathcal{I}$n the limitless desert of love, sensual pleasure has an ardent but very small place, so incandescent that at first one sees nothing else.

COLETTE

*A*las! though we burn with desire without measure
Modesty robs us of all of love's pleasure.

MADAME DE LA SUZE

*L*ove is the word used to label the sexual excitement of the young, the habituation of the middle-aged, and the mutual dependence of the old.

JOHN CIARDI

*L*ove is the only thing you get more of by giving it away.

TOM WILSON

I never liked the men I loved, and I never loved the men I liked.

FANNY BRICE

$\mathcal{I}$ do everything from the heart, from personal conviction. If you try to find love by charting a course, you'll never find it.

VAN CLIBURN

$\mathcal{I}$f you want to read about love and marriage you've got to buy two separate books.

ALAN KING

"$\mathcal{N}$othing, so it seems to me," said the stranger, "is more beautiful than the love that has weathered the storms of life. . . . The love of the young for the young, that is the beginning of life. But the love of the old for the old, that is the beginning of—of things longer."

JEROME K. JEROME,
THE PASSING OF THE THIRD FLOOR BACK

Marriage

$\mathcal{M}$arriage is three parts love and seven parts forgiveness of sins.

LANGDON MITCHELL

$\mathcal{I}$t is not a lack of love, but a lack of friendship that makes unhappy marriages.

FRIEDRICH NIETZSCHE

$\mathcal{M}$arriage is a covered dish.

SWISS PROVERB

$\mathcal{G}$rief often treads upon the heels of pleasure,
Marry'd in haste, we oft repent at leisure;
Some by experience find these words misplaced,
Marry'd at leisure, they repent in haste.

BENJAMIN FRANKLIN

In marriage there is assumed superiority on the part of the husband, and admitted inferiority with a promise of obedience on the part of the wife. This subject calls loudly for examination in order that the wrong may be redressed. Customs suited to darker ages in Eastern countries are not binding upon enlightened society.

LUCRETIA MOTT,
1849

It is a truth . . . universally acknowledged that a single man in possession of a good fortune must be in want of a wife.

JANE AUSTEN

A man should be taller, older, heavier, uglier and hoarser than his wife.

E. W. HOWE

Were kisses all the joys in bed,
One woman would another wed.

WILLIAM SHAKESPEARE

To marry a woman or man for beauty is like buying a
house for its coat of paint.

AMERICAN PROVERB

One can always recognize women who trust their
husbands. They look so thoroughly unhappy.

OSCAR WILDE

I want to be more than a rose in my husband's lapel.

MARGARET TRUDEAU

29

*T*he best part of married life is the fights. The rest is merely so-so.

THORNTON WILDER,
THE MATCHMAKER

*T*he bonds of matrimony are like any other bonds—they mature slowly.

PETER DE VRIES

*M*arriage is a mistake of youth—which we should all make.

DON HEROLD

*H*appiness is being married to your best friend.

T-SHIRT LEGEND

$\mathscr{M}$arriage should be a duet—when one sings, the other claps.

JOE MURRAY

$\mathscr{A}$nyone who watches three games of football in a row should be declared brain dead.

ERMA BOMBECK

$\mathscr{O}$nly choose in marriage a woman whom you would choose as a friend if she were a man.

JOSEPH JOUBERT

$\mathscr{M}$arriage resembles a pair of shears, so joined that they cannot be separated; often moving in opposite directions, yet always punishing any one who comes between them.

SYDNEY SMITH

$\mathcal{I}$f you marry, you will regret it. If you do not marry, you will also regret it.

SOREN KIERKEGAARD

$\mathcal{A}$ happy man marries the girl he loves, but a happier man loves the girl he marries.

ANONYMOUS

$\mathcal{A}$ reformed rake makes the best husband.

PROVERB

$\mathcal{O}$ne good Husband is worth two good wives, for the scarcer things are the more they're valued.

BENJAMIN FRANKLIN

$\mathcal{T}$he best way to get most husbands to do something is to suggest that perhaps they're too old to do it!

ANNE BANCROFT

$\mathcal{D}$o you think your mother and I should have liv'd comfortably so long together, if ever we had been married?

JOHN GAY

$\mathcal{M}$arried life hain't so bad after you git so you kin eat th' things your wife likes.

KIN HUBBARD

$\mathcal{T}$hey dream in courtship, but in wedlock wake.

ALEXANDER POPE

*T*hey stood before the altar and supplied
The fire themselves in which their fat was fried.

AMBROSE BIERCE

I had always thought of my ability to spell "embarrass" as a nice little facility to bring to a marriage—the sort of minor bonus that is sometimes found in a husband's ability to rewire lamps.

CALVIN TRILLIN

I have now come to the conclusion never again to think of marrying, and for this reason: I can never be satisfied with anyone who would be blockhead enough to have me.

ABRAHAM LINCOLN

A misunderstood husband is one whose wife really knows him.

UNKNOWN

Where there's marriage without love, there will be love without marriage.

BENJAMIN FRANKLIN

Chains do not hold a marriage together. It is threads, tiny threads, which sew people together through the years. That is what makes a marriage last—more than passion or sex. It is the threads. . . . But those threads should never become chains.

SIMONE SIGNORET

$\mathcal{Y}$ou can bear your own Faults, and why not a Fault in a Wife?

BENJAMIN FRANKLIN

$\mathcal{T}$he feller that puts off marryin' till he can support a wife ain't very much in love.

KIN HUBBARD

$\mathcal{W}$ho marrieth for love without money hath good nights and sorry days.

ENGLISH PROVERB

I've had diseases that lasted longer than my marriages. You know you are in a bad marriage if you walk down the aisle thinking, "Is this dress right?"

NELL CARTER

*F*irst we make up, and then we fight:
(A miserable wretch am I!)
To live with her's beyond me quite,
And yet without her I should die.

JEAN DESMARETS

*B*efore marriage, a man will lie awake all night thinking about something you said; after marriage, he'll fall asleep before you finish saying it.

HELEN ROWLAND

$\mathcal{A}$ married couple that plays cards together is just a fight that hasn't started yet.

GEORGE BURNS

$\mathcal{T}$here wasn't a wet eye in the place.

JULIE BAUMGOLD,
ABOUT WEDDING OF DONALD TRUMP AND MARLA MAPLES

$\mathcal{T}$he trouble with matrimony is not with the institution, it's with the personnel.

$\mathcal{O}$bserve the face of the wife to know the husband's character.

SPANISH PROVERB

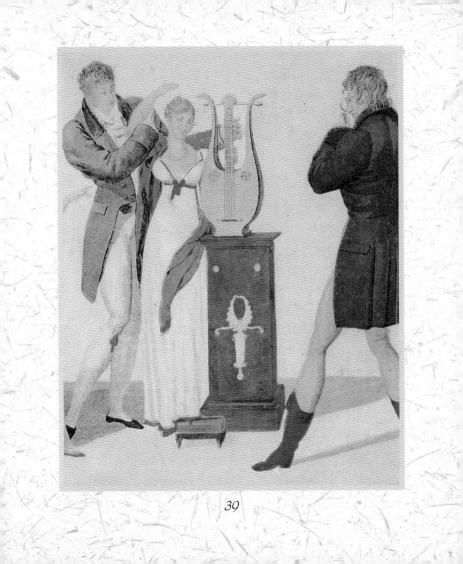

*H*usbands never become good; they merely become proficient.

H. L. MENCKEN

*A*fter all these years, I see that I was mistaken about Eve in the beginning; it is better to live outside the Garden with her than inside it without her.

MARK TWAIN

*I*t is easier to be a lover than a husband, for the simple reason that it is more difficult to have a ready wit the whole day long than to say a good thing occasionally.

HONORÉ DE BALZAC

$\mathcal{A}$ husband is simply a lover with a two-days' growth of beard, his collar off, and a bad cold in his head.

UNKNOWN

$\mathcal{W}$hen widows exclaim loudly against second marriages, I would always lay a wager that the man, if not the wedding day, is absolutely fixed on.

HENRY FIELDING

$\mathcal{I}$ should like to see any kind of a man, distinguishable from a gorilla, that some good and even pretty woman could not shape a husband out of.

OLIVER WENDELL HOLMES

$\mathcal{E}$very man should marry—and no woman.

BENJAMIN DISRAELI

$\mathcal{M}$arriage is a gamble—that's why we speak of winning a husband or wife.

Other men's wives are always the best.

CHINESE PROVERB

$\mathcal{T}$he difficulty with marriage is that we fall in love with a personality, but must live with a character.

PETER DE VRIES

$\mathcal{A}$ man who marries a woman to educate her falls a victim to the same fallacy as the woman who marries a man to reform him.

ELBERT HUBBARD

$\mathcal{A}$ small town is a place where everyone knows whose check is good and whose husband is not.

SID ASCHER

$\mathcal{W}$ithout humor, marriage fails.

LEWIS H. LAPHAM

$\mathcal{T}$he reason most women don't gamble is that their total appetite for gambling is satisfied by marriage.

GLORIA STEINEM

$\mathcal{G}$ive a girl a profession or trade and she will prove that she is a better housewife for this experience, when the right man comes along.

LOUISA LAWSON

$\mathscr{I}$ don't want to send all the married women to work, but what I want is an economic situation where every woman who prefers to be a full-time homemaker and mother may do so, and every woman who wants to be in an outside situation has sufficient, satisfactory childcare available to her so that she can do it without feeling guilty.

DAME BERYL BEAUREPAIRE

$\mathscr{I}$ must admit that there are times when I don't feel particularly in the mood to dress carefully. But I have a husband who always grooms himself in shining fashion the minute he gets up in the morning. You just can't go downstairs in a bathrobe and curlers to face a man who looks like the hero of a soap ad.

IRENE DUNNE,
1939

When we first met and married, he [Bob Dole] felt, definitely, go on with your career. There was never any hesitation. Sure, at times it would have been nice if I could have been at things that were important to him. But we just went forward together.

ELIZABETH DOLE

Heaven will be no heaven to me if I do not meet my wife there.

ANDREW JACKSON

It used to be when we said, "'til death do us part," death parted us pretty soon. That's why marriages used to last forever. Everybody was dead.

MARGARET MEAD

$\mathcal{E}$ven with Lionel at my side, it was my writing which gave the middle years of my life much of their focus and meaning and since his death it is my work which has sustained me at an age when lack of purpose is the death of the living. Difficult as it is to support old age with pride even when one has a loved companion, for a woman alone it is a fierce test of courage; only the luckiest of us have work with which to meet it. In work, especially work at which one has some measure of success, a woman can at least pretend to find a substitute for the sexual power which she must lose with the years.

DIANA TRILLING

$\mathcal{I}$ wasn't allowed to speak while my husband was alive, and since he's gone no one has been able to shut me up.

HEDDA HOPPER

The wooing should be a day after the wedding.

JOHN LYLY

The husband who desires to surprise is often very much surprised himself.

VOLTAIRE

The test of a man or woman's breeding is how they behave in a quarrel.

GEORGE BERNARD SHAW

A good marriage is that in which each appoints the other guardian of his solitude.

RAINER MARIA RILKE

*H*e that tells his wife news is but newly married.

GEORGE HERBERT

*I*f you are afraid of loneliness, don't marry.

ANTON CHEKHOV

I would like to be like my father and all the rest of my ancestors who never married.

MOLIÈRE

*S*ex is better in marriage than anywhere else you can imagine, like the song says: It's all right to get your appetite walking round town just as long as you eat supper at home.

GARRISON KEILLOR,
WE ARE STILL MARRIED

At the beginning of a marriage ask yourself whether this woman will be interesting to talk to from now until old age. Everything else in marriage is transitory: most of the time is spent in conversation.

FRIEDRICH NIETZSCHE

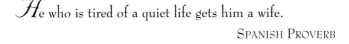

He who is tired of a quiet life gets him a wife.

SPANISH PROVERB

Marriage is the only adventure open to the cowardly.

VOLTAIRE

Here's to matrimony, the high sea for which no compass has yet been invented.

HEINRICH HEINE

$\mathcal{K}$eep your eyes wide open before marriage, and half-shut afterwards.

BENJAMIN FRANKLIN

$\mathcal{T}$here's nothing in the world like the devotion of a married woman. It's a thing no married man knows anything about.

OSCAR WILDE

$\mathcal{E}$very man gets the wife he deserves.

SIMEON B. LAKISH

$\mathcal{I}$'ve been married to one Marxist and one Fascist, and neither one would take the garbage out.

LEE GRANT

*M*y husband will never chase another woman. He's too fine, he's too decent, he's too old.

GRACIE ALLEN

*W*hen money is the bride, the wedding night is cool.

RUSSIAN PROVERB

*T*here is nothing worse than solitude, growing old without a shoulder to lean on. Marry, marry—even if he's fat and boring!

COCO CHANEL

*A*fter you have been married five years, there should always be someone to dinner.

EDWARD LUCAS

*M*arriage is popular because it combines the maximum of temptation with the maximum of opportunity.

GEORGE BERNARD SHAW

*W*hen a divorced man marries a divorced woman, there are four minds in the bed.

TALMUD

*E*asy-crying widows take new husbands soonest; there is nothing like wet weather for transplanting, as Master Gridley used to say.

OLIVER WENDELL HOLMES

A foolish girl may make a lover a husband, but it takes a clever woman to keep a husband a lover.

ED HOWE

*I*f a man cannot distinguish the difference between the pleasures of two consecutive nights, he has married too early in life.

HONORÉ DE BALZAC

*I*t is always incomprehensible to a man that a woman should refuse an offer of marriage.

JANE AUSTEN

A successful marriage requires falling in love many times, always with the same person.

MIGNON MCLAUGHLIN

I have yet to hear a man ask for advice on how to combine marriage and a career.

GLORIA STEINEM

$\mathcal{I}$t is not marriage that fails; it is people that fail. All that marriage does is to show people up.

HARRY EMERSON FOSDICK

$\mathcal{I}$ believe it will be found that those who marry late are best pleased with their children, and those who marry early, with their partners.

SAMUEL JOHNSON

$\mathcal{L}$ove seems the swiftest, but it is the slowest of all growths. No man or woman really knows what perfect love is until they have been married a quarter of a century.

MARK TWAIN

$\mathcal{I}$'m told that times have changed: the New Woman is supposed to be able to fix a carburetor, and the New Couple has a relationship that is modeled not on the relationship between Jimmy Stewart and June Allyson but on the relationship between Butch Cassidy and the Sundance Kid.

CALVIN TRILLIN

$\mathcal{P}$eople are always asking couples whose marriage has endured at least a quarter of a century for their secret for success. Actually, it is no secret at all. I am a forgiving woman. Long ago, I forgave my husband for not being Paul Newman.

ERMA BOMBECK